To

Laura

From

Kay

365 *Smiles a Year For Parents*

365 Smiles a Year For Parents
Copyright © 2006 by FaithPoint Press
Produced by Cliff Road Books

Scripture taken from the HOLY BIBLE: NEW
INTERNATIONAL VERSION®. NIV®. Copyright ©
1973, 1978, 1984 by International Bible Society. Used
by permission of The Zondervan Corporation.

The "NIV" and "New International Version"
trademarks are registered in the United States Patent and
Trademark Office by International Bible Society.
All rights reserved.

ISBN-13: 978-1-58173-573-4
ISBN-10: 1-58173-573-1

Book design by Pat Covert

Printed in China

365 *Smiles a Year* For Parents

It sometimes happens, even in the best of families, that a baby is born. This is not necessarily cause for alarm. The important thing is to keep your wits about you and borrow some money.

Elinor Goulding Smith

❖

Notes: _____

_____

This baby is your blessing. I wish happiness in every way. Good luck, God bless, I say. And many blessings and wishes to welcome baby into your life today.

Unknown

❖

Notes: _____
_____

What are Raphael's Madonnas but the shadow of a mother's love, fixed in a permanent outline forever.

Thomas Wentworth Higginson

❖

Notes: _____
_____

Let parents bequeath to their children not riches, but the spirit of reverence.
Plato

❖

Notes: _____

_____

If you were to open up a baby's head—and I am not for a moment suggesting that you should—you would find nothing but an enormous drool gland.

Dave Barry

❖

Notes: _____

_____

Motherhood has a very humanizing effect. Everything gets reduced to essentials.

Meryl Streep

Notes: _____

_____

January 7

Govern a family as you would cook a small fish, very gently.

Chinese Proverb

❖

Notes: _____

_____

Men are what their mothers
made them.
Ralph Waldo Emerson

❖

Notes: _____
_____

Always end the name of your child with a vowel, so that when you yell, the name will carry.

Bill Cosby

❖

Notes: _____
_____

January 10

There shall never be another quite so tender, quite so kind as the patient little mother. Nowhere on this earth you'll find her affection duplicated.

Paul Brownlow

❖

Notes: _____

_____

Your children tell you casually years later what it would have killed you with worry to know at the time.

Mignon McLaughlin

❖

Notes: _____

_____

A mother understands what a
child does not say.
Jewish Proverb

❖

Notes: _____

_____

Mother's love grows by giving.

Charles Lamb

Notes: _____
_____

A little girl is sugar and spice and everything nice—especially when she's taking a nap.

Unknown

❖

Notes: _____

_____

. . . so that you, your children and their children after them may fear the Lord your God as long as you live by keeping all his decrees and commands that I give you, and so that you may enjoy long life.

Deuteronomy 6:2

❖

Notes: _____

_____

Children are not casual guests in our home. They have been loaned to us temporarily for the purpose of loving them and instilling a foundation of values on which their future lives will be built.

James Dobson

❖

Notes: _____

_____

Only love can be divided endlessly
and still not diminish.

Anne Morrow Lindbergh

❖

Notes: _____

_____

If you want children to keep their feet on the ground, put some responsibility on their shoulders.

Abigail Van Buren

❖

Notes: _____

_____

The quickest way for a parent to get a child's attention is to sit down and look comfortable.

Lane Olinghouse

❖

Notes: _____

_____

There is only one pretty child in the world, and every mother has it.

Chinese Proverb

Notes: _____

_____

Blessed is the influence of one true, loving human soul on another.

George Eliot

❖

Notes: _____

_____

She was the best of all mothers, to whom I owe endless gratitude.

Thomas Carlyle

❖

Notes: _____
_____

Every child born into the world is a new thought of God, an ever fresh and radiant possibility.

Kate Douglas Wiggin

❖

Notes: _____

_____

Love and respect are the most important aspects of parenting, and of all relationships.

Jodie Foster

Notes: _____

_____

Every child comes with the message
that God is not yet discouraged
of man.

Rabindranath Tagore

Notes: _____
_____

Boy, n.: a noise with dirt on it.
Not Your Average Dictionary

❖

Notes: _____

_____

January 27

A mother is a person who, if she is not there when you get home from school, you wouldn't know how to get your dinner, and you wouldn't feel like eating it anyway.

Unknown

❖

Notes: _____
_____

And so our mothers and grandmothers have, more often than not anonymously, handed on the creative spark, the seed of the flower they themselves never hoped to see—or like a sealed letter they could not plainly read.

Alice Walker

❖

Notes: _____
_____

There came a moment quite suddenly a mother realized that a child was no longer hers ... without bothering to ask or even give notice, her daughter had just grown up.

Alice Hoffman

❖

Notes: _____

_____

Loving a child is a circular business … the more you give, the more you get; the more you get, the more you give.

Penelope Leach

Notes: _____
_____

For the mother is and must be,
whether she knows it or not, the
greatest, strongest, and most lasting
teacher her children have.

Hannah W. Smith

❖

Notes: _____
_____

The strength of motherhood is greater than natural laws.

Barbara Kingsolver

❖

Notes: _____

_____

The worst feature of a new baby is its mother's singing.

Kin Hubbard

Notes: _____
_____

No matter how old a mother is, she watches her middle-aged children for signs of improvement.

Florida Scott-Maxwell

❖

Notes: _____

_____

Nothing you do for children is
ever wasted.

Garrison Keillor

❖

Notes: _____

_____

The tie which links mother and child
is of such pure and immaculate
strength as to never be violated.

Washington Irving

❖

Notes: _____

_____

Her dignity consists in being unknown to the world; her glory is in the esteem of her husband; her pleasures in the happiness of her family.

Jean Rousseau

❖

Notes: _____

_____

If I had influence with the good
fairy who is supposed to preside
over the christening of all children, I
should ask that her gift to each child
in the world be a sense of wonder
so indestructible that it would
last throughout life.
Rachel Carson

❖

Notes: _____
_____

A father is someone who carries pictures where his money used to be.

Unknown

❖

Notes: _____
_____

There is none, in all this cold and hollow world, no fount of deep, strong, deathless love, save that within a mother's heart.

Felicia D. Hermans

❖

Notes: _____

_____

Having a baby is definitely
a labor of love.

Joan Rivers

Notes: _____
_____

You may have tangible wealth untold;
Caskets of jewels and coffers of gold.
Richer than I you can never be—
I had a mother who read to me.

Strickland Gillilan

❖

Notes: _____
_____

Loving a child doesn't mean giving in to all his whims; to love him is to bring out the best in him, to teach him to love what is difficult.

Nadia Boulanger

❖

Notes: _____

_____

To show a child what once delighted you, to find the child's delight added to your own, this is happiness.

J. B. Priestley

❖

Notes: _____

_____

In every conceivable manner, the
family is a link to our past,
a bridge to our future.

Alex Haley

❖

Notes: _____
_____

Biology is the least of what makes someone a mother.

Oprah Winfrey

❖

Notes: _____

_____

When I approach a child, he inspires
in me two sentiments: tenderness
for what he is, and respect
for what he may become.

Louis Pasteur

❖

Notes: _____
_____

Children are a great comfort in your old age—and they help you reach it faster, too.
Lionel Kauffman

Notes: _____
_____

Whoever welcomes one of these little children in my name welcomes me; and whoever welcomes me does not welcome me but the one who sent me.

Mark 9:37

❖

Notes: _____

_____

A mother laughs our laughter, Sheds our tears, Returns our love, Fears our fears. She lives our joys, Cares our cares, And all our hopes and dreams she shares.

Julia Summers

❖

Notes: _____

_____

Mother: the essence of loveliness, the beauty of a rose, the sparkle of a dewdrop, and sunset's sweet repose.

Lydia M. Johnson

❖

Notes: _____

_____

The most important thing a father
can do for his children is
to love their mother.

Theodore Hesburgh

❖

Notes: _____

_____

Every mother is like Moses. She does not enter the promised land. She prepares a world she will not see.

Pope Paul VI

❖

Notes: _____

_____

Children are the sum of what
mothers contribute to their lives.

Unknown

Notes: _____

_____

Children seldom misquote you. They more often repeat word for word what you shouldn't have said.

Mae Maloo

Notes: _____
_____

Children are the keys of paradise.
Eric Hoffer

❖

Notes: _____

_____

Sometimes Mom would know what you were thinking before the thought entered your head. "Don't even think about punching your brother," she would warn before you had time to make a fist.

Linda Sunshine

❖

Notes: _____

_____

I long to put the experience of fifty years at once into your young lives, to give you at once the key for that treasure chamber every gem of which has cost me tears and struggles and prayers, but you must work for these inward treasures yourself.

Harriet Beecher Stowe

❖

Notes: _____
_____

Where there is a mother in the home, matters go well.

Amos Bronson Alcott

❖

Notes: _____

_____

Blessed indeed is the man who
hears many gentle voices
call him father!

Lydia Maria Child

❖

Notes: _____
_____

While we try to teach our children all about life, our children teach us what life is all about.

Angela Schwindt

❖

Notes: _____

_____

Babies are always more trouble than you thought—and more wonderful.

Charles Osgood

❖

Notes: _____

_____

The old system of having a baby was much better than the new system, the old system being characterized by the fact that the man didn't have to watch.

Dave Barry

Notes: _____

_____

The memory of my mother and her teachings were, after all, the only capital I had to start life with, and on that capital, I have made my way.

Andrew Jackson

❖

Notes: _____
_____

Before you were conceived, I wanted you. Before you were born, I loved you. Before you were here an hour, I would die for you. This is the miracle of life.

Maureen Hawkins

Notes: _____

_____

Youth fades; love droops; the leaves of friendship fall; a mother's secret hope outlives them all.

Oliver Wendell Holmes Sr.

❖

Notes: _____

_____

A baby is an angel whose wings
decrease as his legs increase.

Unknown

❖

Notes: _____
_____

A mother never realizes that her children are no longer children.

James Agee

❖

Notes: _____

_____

I think that I see something deeper, more infinite, more eternal than the ocean in the expression of the eyes of a little baby when it wakes in the morning and coos or laughs because it sees the sun shining on its cradle.

Vincent van Gogh

❖

Notes: _____

_____

The beauty of "spacing" children many years apart lies in the fact that parents have time to learn the mistakes that were made with the older ones—which permits them to make exactly the opposite mistakes with the younger ones.
Sydney J. Harris

❖

Notes: _____

_____

March 11

All women become like their mothers. That is their tragedy. No man does. That is his.

Oscar Wilde

❖

Notes: _____
_____

The soul is healed by being
with children.
Fyodor Dostoevsky

❖

Notes: _____
_____

I always wanted children, but not until they were actually part of my life did I realize that I could love that fiercely, or get that angry.

Cokie Roberts

❖

Notes: _____

_____

Children who are read to learn two things: First, that reading is worthwhile, and second, that they are worthwhile.

Laura Bush

❖

Notes: _____

_____

March 15

Who ran to help me when I fell, and would some pretty story tell, or kiss the place to make it well?

My mother.

Ann Taylor

Notes: _____

_____

God could not be everywhere,
so He created mothers.
Jewish Proverb

❖

Notes: _____

_____

To nourish children and raise them against odds is in any time, any place, more valuable than to fix bolts in cars or design nuclear weapons.

Marilyn French

❖

Notes: _____

_____

He must manage his own family well and see that his children obey him, and he must do so in a manner worthy of full respect.

1 Timothy 3:4

❖

Notes: _____

_____

Children are the bridge to heaven.

Persian Proverb

Notes: _____

_____

A mother's work is never done.

Unknown

Notes: _____

_____

It is not what you do for your children, but what you have taught them to do for themselves, that will make them successful human beings.

Ann Landers

❖

Notes: _____

_____

There is nothing more thrilling in this world, I think, than having a child that is yours, and yet is mysteriously a stranger.

Agatha Christie

❖

Notes: _____

_____

Children reinvent your world
for you.
Susan Sarandon

Notes: _____
_____

Nobody has ever measured, not even poets, how much the heart can hold.

Zelda Fitzgerald

❖

Notes: _____

_____

The hardest part of raising a child is teaching them to ride bicycles. A shaky child on a bicycle for the first time needs both support and freedom. The realization that this is what the child will always need can hit hard.

Sloan Wilson

❖

Notes: _____

_____

Becoming a mother makes you a grown-up. You're all they have. They trust you; they need you. That's all they want. They want to be loved, protected, and supported.

Celine Dion

❖

Notes: _____

_____

Families with babies and families
without babies are sorry
for each other.

Ed Howe

Notes: _____

_____

Now the thing about having a baby—and I can't be the first person to have noticed this—is that thereafter you have it.

Jean Kerr

Notes: _____

_____

March 29

Women know the way to rear up children (to be just). They know a simple, merry, tender knack of tying sashes, fitting baby shoes, and stringing pretty words that make no sense.

Elizabeth Barrett Browning

❖

Notes: _____
_____

March 30

She made me a security blanket when I was born. That faded green blanket lasted just long enough for me to realize that the security part came from her.

Alexander Crane

❖

Notes: _____
_____

A mother is she who can take the place of all others but whose place no one else can take.

Cardinal Mermillod

❖

Notes: _____
_____

If you bungle raising your children, I don't think whatever else you do matters very much.

Jacqueline Kennedy Onassis

❖

Notes: _____

_____

A mother is the one who is still there when everyone else has deserted you.

Unknown

Notes: _____

_____

April 3

A mother is the truest friend
we have.

Washington Irving

❖

Notes: _____
_____

Grown don't mean nothing to a mother. A child is a child. They get bigger, older, but grown? What's that suppose to mean? In my heart it don't mean a thing.

Toni Morrison

❖

Notes: _____

_____

Children possess a remarkable amount of passion. They throw themselves completely, heart and soul, into everything.

Mary Lou Retton

❖

Notes: _____
_____

I know how to do anything–
I'm a mom.
Roseanne Barr

Notes: _____
_____

The love we give away is the only love we keep.

Elbert Hubbard

❖

Notes: _____

_____

A little girl, asked where her home was, replied, "Where mother is."

Keith L. Brooks

Notes: _____

_____

Love, love, love, that is the soul of genius.

Wolfgang Amadeus Mozart

❖

Notes: _____

_____

It seems to me that my mother was the most splendid woman I ever knew.... I have met a lot of people ... since, but I have never met a more thoroughly refined woman than my mother. If I have amounted to anything, it will be due to her.

Charles Chaplin

❖

Notes: _____

_____

I affirm my profound belief that God's greatest creation is womanhood. I also believe that there is no greater good in all the world than motherhood. The influence of a mother in the lives of her children is beyond calculation.

James E. Faust

❖

Notes: _____

_____

Education commences at the mother's knee, and every word spoken within the hearing of little children tends toward the formation of character.

Hosea Ballou

❖

Notes: _____

_____

Start children off on the way they should go, and even when they are old they will not turn from it.

Proverbs 22: 6

Notes: _____

_____

Whenever I held my newborn baby in my arms, I used to think that what I said and did to him could have an influence not only on him but on all whom he met ... for all eternity—a very challenging and exciting thought for a mother.

Rose Kennedy

❖

Notes: _____

_____

A mother is someone who dreams
great dreams for you, but then she
lets you chase the dreams you have
for yourself and loves you
just the same.

Unknown

❖

Notes: _____

_____

Children are the living messages we send to a time we will not see.

John W. Whitehead

Notes: _____
_____

Life is the first gift, love is the second, and understanding the third.

Marge Piercy

❖

Notes: _____

_____

You don't appreciate your mother until you're a mother yourself.

Catherine Pulsifer

Notes: _____
_____

The babe at first feeds upon the mother's bosom, but it is always on her heart.

Henry Ward Beecher

❖

Notes: _____

_____

People who say they sleep like a baby usually don't have one.

Leo J. Burke

Notes: _____

_____

Having a baby changes the way you view your in-laws. I love it when they come to visit now. They can hold the baby, and I can go out.

Matthew Broderick

❖

Notes: _____

_____

Children and mothers never really
part-bound in the beating
of each other's heart.

Charlotte Gray

❖

Notes: _____
_____

What is a home without children?
Quiet.
Henry Youngman

❖

Notes: _____

_____

My mother loved children—she
would have given anything
if I had been one.

Groucho Marx

Notes: _____

_____

Children represent God's most
generous gift to us.

James Dobson

❖

Notes: _____

_____

The child must know that he is a miracle, that since the beginning of the world there hasn't been, and until the end of the world there will not be, another child like him.

Pablo Casals

❖

Notes: _____
_____

To describe my mother would be to write about a hurricane
in its perfect power.

Maya Angelou

❖

Notes: _____
_____

The mother is queen of that realm
and sways a scepter more potent
than that of kings or priests.

Unknown

❖

Notes: _____

_____

Never fear spoiling children by making them happy. Happiness is the atmosphere in which all good affections grow.

Ann Eliza Bray

❖

Notes: _____

_____

A mother's happiness is like a beacon, lighting up the future but reflected also on the past in the guise of fond memories.

Honoré de Balzac

❖

Notes: _____

_____

The finest inheritance you can give to a child is to allow it to make its own way, completely on its own feet.

Isadora Duncan

❖

Notes: _____

_____

Parents are often so busy with the physical rearing of children that they miss the glory of parenthood, just as the grandeur of the trees is lost when raking leaves.

Marcelene Cox

❖

Notes: _____

_____

One must still have chaos in oneself
to be able to give birth
to a dancing star.

Friedrich Nietzsche

❖

Notes: _____

_____

My mother had a slender, small body, but a large heart—a heart so large that everybody's joys found welcome in it, and hospitable accommodation.

Mark Twain

Notes: _____
_____

When I pick up one of my children and cuddle them, all the strain and stress of life temporarily disappears. There is nothing more wonderful than motherhood, and no one will ever love you as much as a small child.

Nicola Horlick

❖

Notes: _____

_____

Blessed be childhood, which brings down something of heaven into the midst of our rough earthliness.

Henri Frederic Amiel

❖

Notes: _____

_____

A new baby is like the beginning of
all things—wonder, hope,
a dream of possibilities.
Eda J. Le Shan

❖

Notes: _____

_____

It is a wise father who knows
his own child.
William Shakespeare

❖

Notes: _____

_____

She was a genius, my mother.
Sally Kirkland

Notes: _____
_____

Motherhood ... What a glorious career!

Unknown

❖

Notes: _____
_____

Babies are such a nice way to start people.

Don Herrold

Notes: _____

_____

A woman with a child rediscovers the world. All is changed: politics, loyalties, needs. For now all is judged by the life of the child . . . and of all children.

Pam Brown

❖

Notes: _____

_____

My mother wanted me to be her wings, to fly as she never quite had the courage to do. I love her for that. I love the fact that she wanted to give birth to her own wings.

Erica Jong

❖

Notes: _____

_____

All the honest truth-telling in the world is done by children.

Oliver Wendell Holmes Jr.

❖

Notes: _____

_____

A mother always has to think twice,
once for herself and once
for her child.

Sophia Loren

❖

Notes: _____

_____

The noblest calling in the world is that of mother. True motherhood is the most beautiful of all arts, the greatest of all professions.

David O. McKay

❖

Notes: _____

_____

If I were hanged on the highest hill,
Mother o' mine, O mother o' mine! I
know whose love would follow me
still, Mother o' mine,
O mother o' mine!

Rudyard Kipling

❖

Notes: _____

_____

Fathers, do not exasperate your children; instead, bring them up in the training and instruction of the Lord.

Ephesians 6:4

❖

Notes: _____

_____

Motherhood is not for the fainthearted. Frogs, skinned knees, and the insult of teenage girls are not meant for the wimpy.

Danielle Steele

❖

Notes: _____

_____

Children aren't happy with nothing
to ignore, and that's what parents
were created for.

Ogden Nash

❖

Notes: _____
_____

Children in a family are like flowers in a bouquet: There's always one determined to face in an opposite direction from the way the arranger desires.

Marcelene Cox

❖

Notes: _____

_____

If evolution really works, how come mothers only have two hands?

Milton Berle

Notes: _____
_____

A daughter is a little girl who grows up to be a friend.

Unknown

❖

Notes: _____
_____

Harmonizing heart and brain through love … can establish a complete intelligence, a complete self, where a child can look at life and realize there are no dead ends; there are always possibilities. The greatest gift a parent can give a child … is love.

Doc Childre

❖

Notes: _____

_____

If a woman has to choose between catching a fly ball and saving an infant's life, she will choose to save the infant's life without even considering if there are men on base.

Dave Barry

❖

Notes: _____

_____

Mother is the heartbeat in the home, and without her, there seems to be no heart throb.

Leroy Brownlow

Notes: _____

_____

Children are the anchors that hold
a mother to life.
Sophocles

❖

Notes: _____

_____

My mother planted and nurtured the first seeds of good within me. She opened my heart to the lasting impressions of nature; she awakened my understanding and extended my horizon and ... exerted an everlasting influence upon the course of my life.

Immanuel Kant

❖

Notes: _____

_____

It was my mother who taught us to stand up to our problems, not only in the world around us but in ourselves.

Dorothy Pitman Hughes

❖

Notes: _____

_____

Nothing else will ever make you as happy or as sad, as proud or as tired, as motherhood.

Elia Parsons

Notes: _____

_____

My mother is a walking miracle.
Leonardo DiCaprio

❖

Notes: _____
_____

Every baby needs a lap.

Henry Robin

❖

Notes: _____
_____

There is a woman at the beginning of all great things.

Alphonso de Lamartine

❖

Notes: _____

_____

Children, aye forsooth, they bring
their own love with them
when they come.
Jean Ingelow

❖

Notes: _____
_____

A mother is one to whom you hurry
when you are troubled.

Emily Dickinson

❖

Notes: _____
_____

Ten fingers, ten toes. She's laughter and teardrops so small and brand new and amazingly angelic. She's sent to bless you; she's one special baby. The best of life's treasure . . . will grant and bless you many hours of great pleasure.

Unknown

Notes: _____
_____

Perhaps the greatest social service that can be rendered by anybody to the country and to mankind is to bring up a family.

George Bernard Shaw

❖

Notes: _____

_____

The thing that impresses me most about America is the way parents obey their children.

Edward, Duke of Windsor

❖

Notes: _____
_____

Children are likely to live up to what you believe in them.

Lady Bird Johnson

❖

Notes: _____
_____

The voice of parents is the voice of gods, for to their children, they are heaven's lieutenants.

William Shakespeare

❖

Notes: _____

_____

Mother's love is peace. It need not be acquired; it need not be deserved.

Erich Fromm

❖

Notes: _____

_____

And we are put on Earth a little space, that we may learn to bear the beams of love.

William Blake

❖

Notes: _____

_____

She is my Mother, with a capital "M";
she's something sacred to me.

Sophia Loren

❖

Notes: _____
_____

Children learn to smile
from their parents.
Shinichi Suzuki

❖

Notes: _____
_____

Baby: An alimentary canal with a loud voice at one end and no responsibility at the other.

Elizabeth Adamson

❖

Notes: 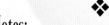 _____

_____

Her caress first awakens in the child a sense of security; her kiss the first realization of affection; her sympathy and tenderness, the first assurance that there is love in the world.

David O. McKay

❖

Notes: _____
_____

Those who spare the rod hate their children, but those who love them are careful to discipline them.

Proverbs 13:24

Notes: _____

_____

A child is a gift whose worth cannot be measured except by the heart.

Theresa Ann Hunt

Notes: _____

_____

I know you've been the best there is—a mother beyond all compare.

Unknown

❖

Notes: _____
_____

The smallest children are nearest to God, as the smallest planets are nearest the sun.

Jean Paul Richter

❖

Notes: _____

_____

There is a religion in all deep love,
but the love of a mother is the veil
of a softer light between the heart
and the heavenly Father.

Samuel Taylor Coleridge

❖

Notes: _____

_____

Getting down on all fours and imitating a rhinoceros stops babies from crying. . . . Keep it up until the kid is a teenager, and he definitely won't have his friends hanging around your house all the time.

P. J. O'Rourke

❖

Notes: _____
_____

Mothers have as powerful an influence over the welfare of future generations as all other earthly causes combined.

John S. C. Abbott

❖

Notes: _____
_____

There are only two lasting bequests we can hope to give our children. One is roots; the other, wings.

Hodding Carter

Notes: _____
_____

Women are aristocrats, and it is always the mother who makes us feel that we belong to the better sort.

John Lancaster Spalding

❖

Notes: _____

_____

A mother takes twenty years to make a man of her boy, and another woman makes a fool of him in twenty minutes.

Robert Frost

❖

Notes: _____

_____

Mother's words of wisdom: "Answer me! Don't talk with food in your mouth!"

Erma Bombeck

❖

Notes: _____

_____

When God thought of mother, He must have laughed with satisfaction, and framed it quickly—so rich, so deep, so divine, so full of soul, power, and beauty, was the conception.

Henry Ward Beecher

❖

Notes: _____
_____

There are three ways to get something done: Do it yourself, employ someone, or forbid your children to do it.

Monta Crane

❖

Notes: _____

_____

You will find as you look back that the moments when you have truly lived are the moments when you have done things in the spirit of love.

Henry Drummond

Notes: _____

_____

There never was a woman like her. She was gentle as a dove and brave as a lioness.

Andrew Jackson

Notes: _____

_____

If a child annoys you, quiet him by brushing his hair. If this doesn't work, use the other end of the brush on the other end of the child.

Unknown

❖

Notes: _____
_____

A mother's love is the fuel that enables a normal human being to do the impossible.

Marion C. Garretty

❖

Notes: _____

_____

There was never a great man who
had not a great mother.
Olive Schreiner

❖

Notes: _____
_____

You don't choose your family. They
are God's gift to you, as
you are to them.
Desmond Tutu

❖

Notes:

I look back on my childhood and thank the stars above. For everything you gave me, but mostly for your love.

Wayne F. Winters

❖

Notes: _____
_____

Who is it that loves me and will love me forever with an affection which no chance, no misery, no crime of mine can do away? It is you, my mother.

Thomas Carlyle

❖

Notes: _____

_____

I think, at a child's birth, if a mother could ask a fairy godmother to endow it with the most useful gift, that gift should be curiosity.

Eleanor Roosevelt

❖

Notes: _____
_____

Adam and Eve had many advantages, but the principal one was that they escaped teething.

Mark Twain

Notes: _____

_____

The mother's heart is the child's schoolroom.

Henry Ward Beecher

Notes: _____
_____

Think of stretch marks as pregnancy service stripes.

Joyce Armor

❖

Notes: _____

_____

Mama was my greatest teacher, a teacher of compassion, love, and fearlessness. If love is sweet as a flower, then my mother is that sweet flower of love.

Stevie Wonder

❖

Notes: _____

_____

And say to mothers what a holy charge is theirs–with what a kingly power their love might rule the fountains of the new-born mind.

Lydia Sigourney

❖

Notes: _____

_____

The family is the nucleus
of civilization.
Will Durant

Notes: _____
_____

When it comes to love,
Mom's the word.

Unknown

❖

Notes: _____
_____

Bear in mind that the wonderful things you learn in your schools are the work of many generations. All this is put in your hands as your inheritance in order that you may receive it, honor it, add to it, and one day faithfully hand it to your children.

Albert Einstein

❖

Notes: _____

_____

Most of all the other beautiful things in life come by twos and threes, by dozens and hundreds. Plenty of roses, stars, sunsets, rainbows, brothers and sisters, aunts and cousins, comrades and friends–but only one mother in the whole world.

Kate Douglas Wiggin

❖

Notes: _____

_____

Some are kissing mothers, and some are scolding mothers, but it is love just the same, and most mothers kiss and scold together.

Pearl S. Buck

❖

Notes: _____

_____

Jesus said, "Let the little children come to me, and do not hinder them, for the kingdom of heaven belongs to such as these."

Matthew 19:14

Notes: _____

_____

A mother is not a person to lean on,
but a person to make leaning
unnecessary.

Dorothy Canfield Fisher

Notes: _____

_____

Every baby born into the world is a finer one than the last.

Charles Dickens

❖

Notes: _____

_____

A woman is the full circle. Within her is the power to create, nurture, and transform.

Diane Mariechild

Notes: _____
_____

Being a mother has made
my life complete.
Darcy Bussell

❖

Notes: _____

_____

A happy childhood is one of the best gifts that parents have it in their power to bestow.

Mary Cholmondeley

Notes: _____

_____

There is no influence so powerful as that of the mother.

Sarah Josepha Hale

❖

Notes: _____

_____

Once upon a memory, someone wiped away a tear, held me close, and loved me.
Thank you, Mother dear.

Unknown

❖

Notes: _____

_____

A baby is a blank cheque made payable to the human race.

Barbara Christine Seifert

❖

Notes: _____
_____

She tried in every way to understand me, and she succeeded. It was this deep, loving understanding as long as she lived that more than anything else helped and sustained me on my way to success.

Mae West

❖

Notes: _____
_____

Women as the guardians of children possess a great power. They are the molders of their children's personalities and the arbiters of their development.

Ann Oakley

❖

Notes: _____

_____

A child's life is like a piece of paper
on which every person
leaves a mark.
Chinese Proverb

❖

Notes: _____
_____

The heart of a mother is a deep abyss at the bottom of which you will always find forgiveness.

Honoré de Balzac

❖

Notes: _____

_____

The greatest lessons I have ever learned were at my mother's knees. . . . All that I am, or hope to be, I owe to my angel mother.

Abraham Lincoln

❖

Notes: _____
_____

As a mother, my job is to take care
of what is possible and trust God
with the impossible.

Ruth Bell Graham

Notes: _____

_____

One lamp—thy mother's love—amid the stars/ Shall lift its pure flame changeless, and before/ The throne of God, burn through eternity—/ Holy—as it was lit and lent thee here.

Nathaniel Parker Willis

❖

Notes: _____

_____

It will be gone before you know it.
The fingerprints on the wall appear
higher and higher. Then suddenly
they disappear.

Dorothy Evslin

❖

Notes: _____

_____

No one in the world can take the
place of your mother.

Harry S. Truman

Notes: _____
_____

The human heart feels things the eyes cannot see and knows what the mind cannot understand.

Robert Vallett

❖

Notes: _____

_____

The best thing you can give children,
next to good habits,
are good memories.
Sydney J. Harris

❖

Notes: _____
_____

The trouble with being a parent is that by the time you are experienced, you are unemployed.

Unknown

❖

Notes: _____
_____

Children are the hands by which we take hold of heaven.

Henry Ward Beecher

Notes: _____

_____

If we don't stand up for children,
then we don't stand up for much.

Marian Wright Edelman

❖

Notes: _____
_____

All the earth, though it were full of kind hearts, is but a desolation and a desert place to a mother when her only child is absent.

Elizabeth Gaskell

❖

Notes: _____
_____

I love my mother dearly, but it wouldn't be suitable for me to live with her all the time.

Keith Emerson

❖

Notes: _____
_____

One of the most obvious results of having a baby around the house is to turn two good people into complete idiots who probably wouldn't have been much worse than mere imbeciles without it.

Georges Courteline

❖

Notes: _____

_____

In the sheltered simplicity of the first days after a baby is born, one sees again the magical closed circle, the miraculous sense of two people existing only for each other.

Anne Morrow Lindbergh

❖

Notes: _____
_____

When the first baby laughed for the first time, the laugh broke into a thousand pieces, and they all went skipping about.

Sir James M. Barrie

❖

Notes: _____
_____

A rod and a reprimand impart wisdom, but children left to themselves disgrace their mother.

Proverbs 29:15

❖

Notes: _____

_____

Romance fails us and so do friendships, but the relationship of parent and child, less noisy than all the others, remains indelible and indestructible, the strongest relationship on earth.

Theodore Reik

❖

Notes: _____

_____

You don't really understand human nature unless you know why a child on a merry-go-round will wave at his parents every time around—and why his parents will always wave back.

William D. Tammeus

❖

Notes: _____
_____

Parents often talk about the younger generation as if they didn't have anything to do with it.

Haim Ginott

❖

Notes: _____
_____

Motherhood is priced of God, at a price no man may dare to lessen or misunderstand.

Helen Hunt Jackson

Notes: _____

_____

A mother's children are
portraits of herself.

Unknown

❖

Notes: _____
_____

A baby is an inestimable blessing
and bother.

Mark Twain

Notes: _____
_____

In all my efforts to learn to read, my mother shared fully my ambition and sympathized with me and aided me in every way she could. If I have done anything in life worth attention, I feel sure that I inherited the disposition from my mother.

Booker T. Washington

❖

Notes: _____
_____

My mom used to say it didn't matter how many kids you have . . . because one kid'll take up 100% of your time, so more kids can't possibly take up more than 100%
of your time.

Karen Brown

❖

Notes: _____
_____

So for the mother's sake, the child was dear, and dearer was the mother for the child.

Samuel Taylor Coleridge

❖

Notes: _____

_____

A baby is born with a need to be loved and never outgrows it.

Frank A. Clark

Notes: _____

_____

The role of mother is probably the most important career a woman can have.

Janet Mary Riley

❖

Notes: _____
_____

It was the tiniest thing I ever decided to put my whole life into.

Terri Guillemets

❖

Notes: _____

_____

She is my first, great love.
D. H. Lawrence

❖

Notes: _____

_____

The hand that rocks the cradle is the hand that rules the world.

William Ross Wallace

❖

Notes: _____

_____

Thou art thy mother's glass, and she in thee calls back the lovely April of her prime.

William Shakespeare

Notes: _____
_____

The decision to have a child is to accept that your heart will forever walk about outside of your body.

Katherine Hadley

❖

Notes: _____

_____

The best way to make children good
is to make them happy.

Oscar Wilde

❖

Notes: _____

_____

The best medicine in the world
is a mother's kiss.
Unknown

❖

Notes: _____
_____

A debt so large and special, the like
there is no other, this debt and so
much very more, we owe
it to our mother!

Bill Ronan

❖

Notes: _____

_____

I love being a mother.... I am more aware. I feel things on a deeper level. I have a kind of understanding about my body, about being a woman.

Shelley Long

❖

Notes: _____

_____

Love is the greatest refreshment
in life.
Pablo Picasso

❖

Notes: _____
_____

When you put faith, hope, and love together, you can raise positive kids in a negative world.

Zig Ziglar

❖

Notes: _____

_____

As a parent, you try to maintain a certain amount of control, and so you have this tug-of-war.... You have to learn when to let go. And that's not easy.

Aretha Franklin

Notes: _____

_____

The mother loves her child most divinely, not when she surrounds him with comfort and anticipates his wants, but when she resolutely holds him to the highest standards and is content with nothing less than his best.

Hamilton W. Mabie

❖

Notes: _____

_____

God's interest in the human race is
nowhere better evinced
than in obstetrics.

Martin H. Fischer

Notes: _____
_____

A sweet child is the sweetest

thing in nature.

Charles Lamb

❖

Notes: _____

_____

Motherhood: All love begins
and ends there.

Robert Browning

❖

Notes: _____
_____

A mother's arms are made of tenderness, and children sleep soundly in them.

Victor Hugo

Notes: _____

_____

Oh what a power is mother,
possessing a potent spell.

Euripides

Notes: _____

_____

Even when freshly washed and relieved of all obvious confections, children tend to be sticky.

Fran Lebowitz

Notes: _____

_____

Take a sprinkling of fairy dust, an angel's single feather. Also a dash of love and care, then mix them both together. Add a sentiment or two, a thoughtful wish or line. A touch of stardust, a sunshine ray. It's a recipe, for a Baby Girl truly fine.

Unknown

❖

Notes: _____

_____

It's frightening to think that you mark your children merely by being yourself. It seems unfair. You can't assume the responsibility for everything you do—or don't do.

Simone de Beauvoir

❖

Notes: _____

_____

When we love anyone with our whole hearts, life begins when we are with that person; it is only in their company that we are really and truly alive.

William Barclay

❖

Notes: _____

_____

Children are a heritage from the
Lord, offspring a reward from him.

Psalms 127:3

❖

Notes: _____

_____

It kills you to see them grow up. But I guess it would kill you quicker if they didn't.

Barbara Kingsolver

❖

Notes: _____
_____

Mother's Day is in honor of the best
Mother who ever lived—the
Mother of your heart.

Anna Jarvis

Notes: _____

_____

What feeling is so nice as a child's hand in yours? So small, so soft and warm, like a kitten huddling in the shelter of your clasp.

Marjorie Holmes

❖

Notes: _____

_____

A baby is God's opinion that the world should go on.

Carl Sandburg

❖

Notes: _____

_____

Who takes the child by the hand
takes the mother by the heart.

German Proverb

Notes: _____

_____

I miss thee, my Mother! Thy image is
still the deepest impressed
on my heart.

Eliza Cook

❖

Notes: _____

_____

September 25

It would seem that something which means poverty, disorder, and violence every single day should be avoided entirely, but the desire to beget children is a natural urge.

Phyllis Diller

❖

Notes: _____
_____

A child enters your home, and for the next twenty years makes so much noise you can hardly stand it. The child departs, leaving the house so silent you think you are going mad.

John Andrew Holmes

❖

Notes: _____
_____

A child's hand in yours—what tenderness and power it arouses. You are instantly the very touchstone of wisdom and strength.

Marjorie Holmes

❖

Notes: _____

_____

Don't limit a child to your own learning, for he was born in another time.

Unknown

❖

Notes: _____

_____

The mother is the most precious possession of the nation, so precious that society advances its highest well-being when it protects the functions of the mother.

Ellen Key

Notes: _____
_____

In the evening, after she has gone to sleep, I kneel beside the crib and touch her face, where it is pressed against the slats, with mine.

Joan Didion

❖

Notes: _____
_____

Mother: the most beautiful word on the lips of mankind.

Kahlil Gibran

Notes: _____

_____

Sometimes the poorest woman
leaves her children the
richest inheritance.
Ruth E. Renkel

Notes: _____

_____

Who, being loved, is poor?
Oscar Wilde

❖

Notes: _____
_____

Motherhood is the greatest potential influence in human society.

David O. McKay

❖

Notes: _____

_____

Little children are still the symbol of the eternal marriage between love and duty.

George Eliot Romola

Notes: _____
_____

Cherishing children is the mark
of a civilized society.

Joan Ganz Cooney

❖

Notes: _____
_____

Never raise your hand to your children; it leaves your midsection unprotected.

Miriam Robbins

❖

Notes: _____

_____

When a child enters the world through you, it alters everything on a psychic, psychological, and purely practical level.

Jane Fonda

❖

Notes: _____

_____

We find delight in the beauty and happiness of children that make the heart too big for the body.

Ralph Waldo Emerson

Notes: _____

_____

A rich child often sits in a poor mother's lap.

Danish Proverb

❖

Notes: _____

_____

No painter's brush, nor poet's pen
In justice to her fame
Has ever reached half high enough
To write a mother's name.
Unknown

❖

Notes: _____
_____

Family has always been the most important thing in my life. The only real goal that I ever had was to be a good mother.

Goldie Hawn

❖

Notes: _____

_____

October 13

The mother-child relationship is very paradoxical. It requires the most intense love on the mother's side, yet this very love must help the child grow away from the mother and become fully independent.

Erich Fromm

❖

Notes: _____

_____

Discovering that with every child, your heart grows bigger and stronger—that there is no limit to how much or how many people you can love, even though at times you feel as though you could burst—you don't—you just love even more.
Yasmin Le Bon

❖

Notes: _____
_____

Children are the true connoisseurs.
What's precious to them has
no price, only value.

Bel Kaufman

Notes: _____

_____

It is easier to build strong children
than to repair broken men.
Frederick Douglas

❖

Notes: _____

_____

Woman knows what man has long forgotten, that the ultimate economic and spiritual unit of any civilization is still the family.

Clara Boothe Luce

❖

Notes: _____

_____

I have found the best way to give advice to your children is to find out what they want and then advise them to do it.

Harry S. Truman

❖

Notes: _____

_____

A mother has, perhaps, the hardest earthly lot, and yet no mother worthy of the name ever gave herself thoroughly for her child who did not feel that, after all, she reaped what she had sown.

Henry Ward Beecher

❖

Notes: _____

_____

If a child is to keep alive his inborn sense of wonder, he needs the companionship of at least one adult who can share it, rediscovering with him the joy, excitement, and mystery of the world we live in.

Rachel Carson

❖

Notes: _____

_____

October 21

It takes a village to raise a child.

African Proverb

❖

Notes: _____

_____

Children's children are a crown to the aged, and parents are the pride of their children.

Proverbs 17:6

Notes: _____

_____

A mother's love is patient and forgiving when all others are forsaking, and it never fails or falters, even though the heart is breaking.

Helen Steiner Rice

❖

Notes: _____

_____

A baby will make love stronger, days shorter, nights longer, bankroll smaller, home happier, clothes shabbier, the past forgotten, and the future worth living for.

Unknown

Notes: _____
_____

Kids are life's only guaranteed,
bona fide upside surprise.

Jack Nicholson

❖

Notes: _____

_____

The sweetest sounds to mortals given are heard in Mother, Home, and Heaven.

William Goldsmith Brown

Notes: _____

_____

A mother is a mother still, the holiest thing alive.

Samuel Taylor Coleridge

❖

Notes: _____

_____

Mother is the name of God in the lips and hearts of children.

William Thackeray

❖

Notes: _____

_____

Because I feel that in the heavens above, the angels, whispering one to another, can find among their burning tears of love, none so devotional as that of "Mother."

Edgar Allan Poe

❖

Notes: _____

_____

When motherhood becomes the fruit of a deep yearning, not the result of ignorance or accident, its children will become the foundation of a new race.

Margaret Sanger

❖

Notes: _____

_____

My opinion is that the future good
or bad conduct of a child depends
on its mother.

**Letizia Ramolino Bonaparte,
Napoleon's mother**

❖

Notes: _____
_____

This would be a better world for
children if parents had
to eat the spinach.

Groucho Marx

❖

Notes: _____
_____

My mother was the most beautiful woman I ever saw.

George Washington

❖

Notes: _____

_____

Of all the rights of women, the greatest is to be a mother.

Lin Yutang

Notes: _____

_____

To be a mother is a woman's greatest vocation in life. She is a partner with God. No being has a position of such power and influence. She holds in her hands the destiny of nations, for to her comes the responsibility . . . of molding the nation's citizens.

Spencer W. Kimball

❖

Notes: _____

_____

The mother love is like God's love;
He loves us not because we are
lovable, but because it is His nature
to love, and because we
are His children.

Earl Riney

❖

Notes: _____
_____

A mother holds her children's hands
for a while, their hearts forever.

Unknown

Notes: _____

_____

My hope for my children must be
that they respond to the still, small
voice of God in their own hearts.

Andrew Young

❖

Notes: _____
_____

Happy he with such a mother! Faith in womankind beats with his blood.

Alfred, Lord Tennyson

Notes: _____

_____

Your children need your presence
more than your presents.

Jesse Jackson

Notes: _____
_____

There never was a child so lovely
but his mother was glad
to get him asleep.

Ralph Waldo Emerson

Notes: _____

_____

Parents can only give good advice or put them on the right paths, but the final forming of a person's character lies in their own hands.

Anne Frank

❖

Notes: _____

_____

Mothers are the pivot on
which the family spins.
Pam Brown

Notes: _____
_____

The trouble with children is that they are not returnable.

Fyodor Dostoyevski

❖

Notes: _____
_____

And it came to me, and I knew what I had to have before my soul would rest. I wanted to belong–to belong to my mother. And in return–I wanted my mother to belong to me.

Gloria Vanderbilt

❖

Notes: _____

_____

My first vivid memory is . . . when first I looked into her face and she looked into mine. That I do remember, and that exchanging looks I have carried with me all of my life. We recognized each other. I was her child, and she was my mother.

Pearl S. Buck

❖

Notes: _____
_____

Children require guidance and
sympathy far more than instruction.

Annie Sullivan

❖

Notes: _____
_____

The family is one of
nature's masterpieces.
George Santayana

❖

Notes: _____

_____

If you have the courage to touch life for the first time, you will never know what hit you. Everything man has thought, felt, and experienced is gone, and nothing is put in its place.

U. G. Krishnamurti

❖

Notes: _____

_____

I stood in the hospital corridor the night after she was born. Through a window I could see all the ... newborn infants, and somewhere among them slept ... mine. I stood ... for hours filled with happiness until the night nurse sent me to bed.

Liv Ullman

❖

Notes: _____

_____

The joys of motherhood are never
fully experienced until
the children are in bed.

Unknown

❖

Notes: _____

_____

All your children will be taught
by the Lord, and great will
be their peace.
Isaiah 54:13

❖

Notes: _____

_____

Forgiveness is the answer to the
child's dream of a miracle by which
what is broken is made whole
again, what is soiled is
again made clean.

Dag Hammarsjold

❖

Notes: _____
_____

Bitter are the tears of a child: sweeten them. Deep are the thoughts of a child: quiet them. Sharp is the grief of a child: take it from him. Soft is the heart of a child: do not harden it.

Pamela Glenconnor

❖

Notes: _____

_____

A mother is a person who, seeing there are only four pieces of pie for five people, promptly announces she never did care for pie.

Tenneva Jordan

❖

Notes: _____
_____

Kindness in words creates confidence. Kindness in thinking creates profoundness. Kindness in giving creates love.
Lao Tzu

❖

Notes: _____

_____

If pregnancy were a book, they would cut the last two chapters.

Nora Ephron

Notes: _____
_____

The best training any parent can give
a child is to train the child
to train himself.

A. P. Gouthey

Notes: _____

_____

Who in their infinite wisdom
decreed that Little League uniforms
be white? Certainly not a mother.

Erma Bombeck

❖

Notes: _____
_____

You will always be your
child's favorite toy.
Vicki Lansky

❖

Notes: _____

_____

Becoming responsible adults is no longer a matter of whether children hang up ... pajamas or put ... towels in the hamper, but whether they care about themselves and others–and whether they see ... chores as related to how we treat this planet.

Eda J. Le Shan

❖

Notes: _____

_____

Furnish an example, stop preaching, stop shielding, don't prevent self-reliance and initiative, allow your children to develop along their own lines.

Eleanor Roosevelt

❖

Notes: _____
_____

The only thing worth stealing is a kiss from a sleeping child.

Joe Houldsworth

❖

Notes: _____

_____

The heart that loves is
always young.
Unknown

Notes: _____

_____

The phrase "working mother"
is redundant.

Jane Sellman

Notes: _____
_____

I never thought that you should be rewarded for the greatest privilege of life.

Mary Roper Coker, Mother of the Year 1958

❖

Notes: _____

_____

The moment a child is born, the mother is also born.

Rajneesh

❖

Notes: _____

_____

You can learn many things from children. How much patience you have, for instance.

Franklin P. Jones

Notes: _____

_____

Love still has something of the sea
From whence his mother rose.

Sir Charles Sedley

❖

Notes: _____

_____

She never quite leaves her children at home, even when she doesn't take them along.

Margaret Culkin Banning

❖

Notes: _____
_____

All that I am, my mother made me.
John Quincy Adams

❖

Notes: _____
_____

A babe in a house is a well-spring
of pleasure, a messenger
of peace and love.

Martin Farquhar Tupper

Notes: _____

_____

All mothers are rich when they love
their children. Their love is always
the most beautiful of joys.

Maurice Maeterlinck

❖

Notes: _____

_____

Life began with waking up and loving my mother's face.

George Eliot

❖

Notes: _____
_____

My mother was the making of me. She was so true and so sure of me, I felt that I had someone to live for— someone I must not disappoint. The memory of my mother will always be a blessing to me.

Thomas A. Edison

❖

Notes: _____

_____

I cannot forget my mother. She is my bridge. When I needed to get across, she steadied herself long enough for me to run across safely.

Renita Weems

❖

Notes: _____
_____

Nothing has a better effect upon children than praise.

Sir Philip Sidney

❖

Notes: _____

_____

An ounce of mother is worth
a ton of priest.

Spanish Proverb

❖

Notes: _____

_____

I have no greater joy than to hear
that my children are walking
in the truth.
3 John 1:4

Notes: _____

_____

Mothers are instinctive philosophers.

Harriet Beecher Stowe

❖

Notes: _____

_____

To a child's ear, "mother" is magic in any language.
Arlene Benedict

Notes: _____

_____

A child is the root of the heart.

Carolina Maria de Jesus

❖

Notes: _____
_____

Mother–that was the bank where
we deposited all our hurts
and worries.

T. DeWitt Talmage

❖

Notes: _____

_____

The bearing and the training of a child is woman's wisdom.

Alfred, Lord Tennyson

❖

Notes: _____

_____

There is no friendship, no love, like that of the parent for the child.

Henry Ward Beecher

❖

Notes: _____

_____

Every child born has
innate goodness.
Chinese Proverb

❖

Notes: _____

_____

A woman can learn a lot from holding a new baby. It is life beginning again—sweet possibilities! No problem in the world is big enough to be remembered.

Susan McOmber

❖

Notes: _____
_____

If you raise your children to feel that they can accomplish any goal or task they decide upon, you will have succeeded as a parent, and you will have given your children the greatest of all blessings.

Brian Tracy

❖

Notes: _____
_____

To the world, each one of us may be just one small person, but to one small person, we may be the world.

Unknown

❖

Notes: _____

_____

Parenthood: That state of being better chaperoned than you were before marriage.

Marcelene Cox

❖

Notes: _____

_____

As much as we watch to see what our children do with their lives, they are watching us to see what we do with ours. I can't tell my children to reach for the sun. All I can do is reach for it, myself.

Joyce Maynard

❖

Notes: _____

_____

A mother's love for her child is like nothing else in the world. It knows no law, no pity, it dares all things and crushes down remorselessly all that stands in its path.

Agatha Christie

❖

Notes: _____
_____